"When watching a loved one die slowly — over a span of months or years — the five stages of grief don't wait around for that final breath. Even so, we're never ready, even when we are. *It was too late*, Ken Gierke writes. *For all of us, it was too early.* The long passing of a parent, someone who's passed on half of our DNA, carries with it a sixth stage: Waiting for our bodies to betray us as well. Gierke's *The Long Haul* captures that somber matter-of-factness through three narrative threads: The death of Gierke's father, his own yearlong health crisis when his gallbladder went bad, and a congenital hole in a wall of his heart. He recounts each in small telling details: a panhandler near his father's hospital, stubbed toes turning blue, the sound of Miles Davis' horn as the last of the anesthesia wears off. The poems here acknowledge grief, apprehension, pain physical and psychic. They do not, however, wallow in them. *The Long Haul* lives in those fifth and sixth stages — and are far more affecting and effective for that. When Gierke writes *Nothing to do but let it play / until the clock runs down,* we set our mouths and nod along with him. We have been there, we are there, and we and our loved ones will be there sooner or later."

-Steve Brisendine, author, *Pitch Invader on a Foosball Table* and *Behind the Wall Cloud of Sleep*

"This book is a family affair and we learn the journey we are on is never completed even after decades have passed, even if our secrets, expectations, and obligations are buried in the backyard garden waiting for the next resurrection. And we learn that life takes a lifetime for all the body's failures to coalesce, and become a place that he can hold onto until he can't and hello becomes goodbye.

The Long Haul by Ken Gierke is a love story. All of us are born here by a mother and father. Ken's father taught him to confront life, not to surrender, not to back away. There is nothing that is definite, determined, lasting. Ken learns that life is relative, changing, growing, following up and down in expected and unexpected paths. There is always something to share, someone to thank and he does thank his father for his guidance many times."

-Walter Bargen, first Poet Laureate of Missouri and author of *Orwell at the Kremlin*

The Long Haul

Poems by Ken Gierke

Spartan Press

Kansas City, Missouri

Copyright © Ken Gierke, 2026

First Edition: 1 3 5 7 9 10 8 6 4 2

ISBN: 979-8-89975-039-7

LCCN: 2026937541

Cover image: Doris Darlak-Gierke

Title page image: Ken Gierke

Author photo: Donna Gierke

Acknowledgments

Special thanks go to the editors of the following publi-cations where these poems first appeared:

MasticadoresUSA: "Missed in Any Weather"
Well Versed: "Missed Beat"
The Rye Whiskey Review: "One Hit Wonder"
SHINE Quarterly: "Don't Lose Heart"
Literary Revelations: "Wayback Machine" and "Road to Recovery"
LatinosUSA: "Freddie Freeloader"
As It Ought to Be Magazine: "Dulcet Tones Do Not Lessen the Impact"
Chamomile Zine: "A Face Well Known"
Well Versed: "Designated Driver"

Table of Contents

Effortlessly

It seems I only see you
when you come into my dreams.

I hear words, conversations,
remember what I learned back then.

Lessons never seemed to be lessons
when working by your side.

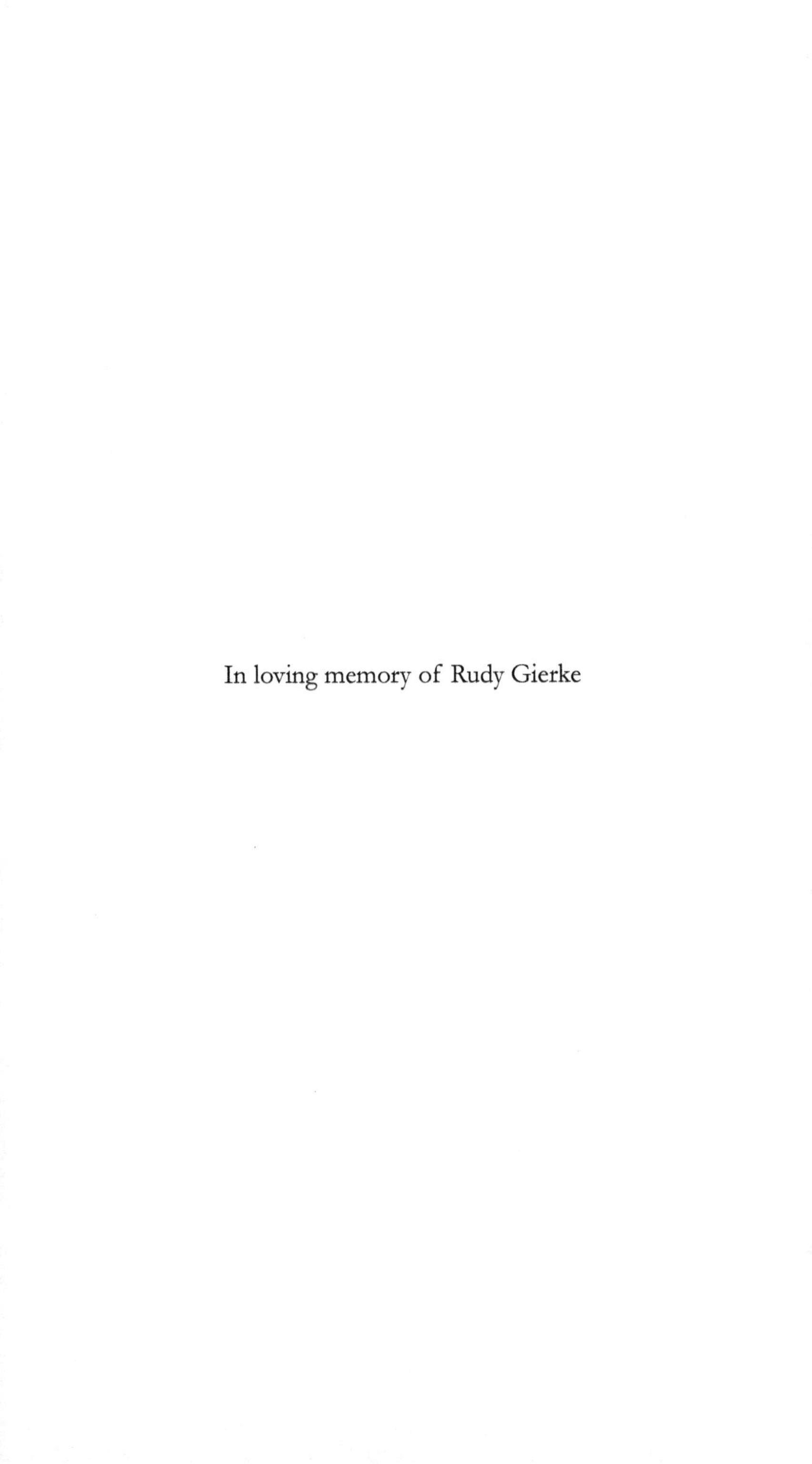

In loving memory of Rudy Gierke

random admission

i hear voices

like a dream
trying to break
through

words
wedged between,
within, around
words strangle
what's known

until it's not

a sleepwalker's nightmare
of internal conversation,
voices better
left to themselves

incoherence
rising above
the ears' eternal howl,
battling for acknowledgment
in a waking world

better left to itself

not worth the risk

Relativity

Out of winter's cold and into the hospital, how
could there be anything but warmth? Still, a
greater chill comes over me, and my breath is
sucked out of me as I pause at the door to the
corridor. Only nine, maybe ten, this girl before
me, tucked into a wheelchair with a blanket, her
head wrapped so that no hair is visible. Is there
any?

My warning to brace for the cold as I hold
the door open is met with her mother's wan
smile, but the child's laughter is a reminder that
hardship, sorrow, and joy are relative to each of us.
Perspective takes a bow when least expected, but
when needed most, and I'm flooded with warmth.

Ripe Tomato at 3 pm

Not a meal, but a Saturday treat.
Heirloom, of course, ripe with memories.
Savoring the process of your hand moving,
slow and smooth, the serrated knife laying
each slice on the bread, each slice layered
with mayo turning pink with juice.
Now held in two hands, that second slice
firmly in place, mayo in a bead, hugging
the crust edge, juice falling to the plate
in languid drops. Eyes closed with each bite,
you relish this simple pleasure.
My pleasure now in recalling this,
bringing you back after so many years
as I take my own bite and savor the memory.

Memories on the Downslope

It was winter, early 1966.
Do you remember where?
Of course you would,
but you're no longer here to say.

Somewhere in Pennsylvania.
A grandparents' farm, family friends.
We camped there several times,
but for that visit we stayed in the farmhouse.

All for a fun day of sledding for the kids.
Why shouldn't a dad join in?
Diving onto that wood and metal glider
you raced down the hill, unstoppable.

Until you found the one bare spot
on that long slope of a farm field.
The sled came to a dead halt,
but you rocketed forward.

We found your metal frame glasses coated
with blood from the gash in your brow.
Just like that, the cold seeped into all of us,
so we went inside while you were taped up.

But the day was early, and our bones
were warmed by hot chocolate,

so we loaded up the grandparents' van,
ten of us packed into a '64 Econoline.

We headed for an old logging road,
snow covered and perfect for sledding.
Of course, you were more than content
to let the kids have all the fun.

Sugar Rush

Cakes and pies?
Of course, but always ice cream.
Except when there wasn't.
Doctor's appointment the next week.
Back in the sixties,
that's the only time
they measured blood sugar.
Didn't want it high for the test.
Back to ice cream, after.
Thirty years later,
that was a losing bet.

Work, as an Ethic

It was 1973.
My car would be in the want ads in two days.
Big problem.
Like throwing a switch, the transmission was shot.

You said, "Well, it's not going to fix itself."

Off to the junkyard, for a used transmission.
Across the street, a transmission jack at a tool rental.
Four hours and $75 later, drove like a charm.
Two days later, sold for $200.

You said, "Better than $25 for scrap, right?"

Blue collar child of the Depression.
Working full-time from the age of thirteen.
Little sense in living beyond your means.
If wanting more meant working for it, then so be it.

You taught me that, and so much more.

Country Roads

Scent of campfire still in my clothes,
I woke to the smell of bacon,
eggs, and coffee, and rushed out
to hear my father laughing at
my enthusiasm. A camping trip,
country roads, and driving lessons.

When Dad decided desolate roads
with few distractions were perfect
for my first time, I jumped at the chance.
Learner's permit burning a hole in my pocket,
I could already feel my hands on the wheel.

As we sat on the side of the road,
he covered each feature before me.
Speedometer. Gauges. Signals.
Hand placement. Each instruction
repeated back to him.

Once I put that '64 Olds into gear
and gently pressed the accelerator,
I eased onto the road. He reminded me
to take a little less time on the shoulder.
Four tires on the road were better than two.

Intimidated by the first oncoming car,
I moved to the right and made sure

to stay closer to the shoulder. I swear
he ducked as we passed a mailbox
and he strongly suggested
I stay in the center of my lane.

One blemish on an otherwise perfect day.
Around the campfire that evening,
we talked about driving. He even agreed
I could get a motorcycle,
once I had the money for one.

He taught me well.
Driver's ed was just a formality.
Insurance discount. More than once
over the years, he said he was proud of
my driving skills. From cars to motorcycles
to semis, it all started on those country roads.

Designated Driver

stopped car ahead
swerve hard left
hard right, back into lane
front wheel dances
in slow-mo at 50 mph
bike takes forever
to slide to its side
my knee dents the fuel tank
I hit the pavement
in time with the handlebars
head first, headlight first
minor damage there
helmet bounces, grinding
away for a quarter-inch
denim jacket shredded
at the shoulder, hip
introduced to road rash
as my belt is ripped
and jeans are worn through
going down the road
facing that bike, cursing
up a storm on a sunny day
until we come to a stop,
my slightly damaged bike
and my battered and concussed
body waiting for the ambulance
where I tell the EMT
I think I can drive home

Shoulder Your Responsibilities

Arm yourself.
Leverage the weight
you carry against the wait
imposed by a system
that places a percentage
on disability, your inability
to function notwithstanding.
Security in your social setting
won't come easy. For most,
it takes several tries.
Hire a lawyer.
Tack a cardiac event onto it.
Maybe a few bypasses.
And when you get that card,
hold on to it with your life.

Dive Buddy

CPR class at Red Cross
Part of my scuba training
Rescue Diver Certification

Learned something new
A sore jaw could be
an indication of a heart attack

That evening, call Mom and Dad
Ask how their Florida trip went
Dad's been resting for hours

Won't get up
Can't figure out why
his jaw hurts so much

It's a heart attack — call 911
I don't think he wants me to
Call, anyway!

Transport to local hospital
Another ambulance to Buffalo
Five coronary bypasses

Dad made scuba possible, helped
to buy my first scuba gear
It saved his life

Together for the Long Haul

Crossing the Genesee River,
front tire of my motorcycle
squiggling in a slow crawl
across the steel deck bridge.
Just part of the trip,
till they replaced it.

The giant girders and stanchions
from the train bridge
that crossed your valley
lying beside the road,
waiting to be hauled away
while we worked on projects,
improved the five acres
waiting for your retirement.

Riding home, wind in my face
as I followed you pulling
your empty trailer back home,
when the rear tire on my bike
blew out and I wove to a stop.
Five minutes later, you turned
around to find me sitting
on a porch while I waited for you.

We pushed the bike up onto
the trailer and hauled it home,

one more project to strengthen
the connection we'd had
since you and Mom
first brought me home.

reassurance

no 2 ways about it
more like 5
bypasses
after 50+ years of
bad habits

out in 5 days
right back in
for another 5
out once more
feeling like $1M

now worried about her
the heart of the matter
under the knife
ribcage cracked open
one more bond they share

no getting around it
the difference here
a mitral valve
faulty for a lifetime
now mechanical

ear pressed to her breast
methodic ticking
brings reassurance

Double or Nothing

When a sore jaw
is more than a sore jaw,
a quintuple bypass soon follows.
Standard recovery,
too short by reasonable standards.
Immediate follow-up on release.
Ever seen your father's heart
as it beats on the screen in front of you?
Seen the look on a doctor's face
when he gets the results?
Immediate readmission
to a hospital closer to home.
The insurance game,
to allow full recovery.
A recovery
that was all for nothing
ten years later, in Vegas.
A double bypass
that didn't quite get him home.

As the Pale Moon Rises

An autumn night, and the pale moon rises.
My mind goes back as the pale moon rises.

To a man in the autumn of his life,
In autumn days as the pale moon rises.

With talk of work that's done and left to do.
A day well spent as the pale moon rises.

Having no regrets, taking stock of life
And what's in store as the pale moon rises.

In quiet moments under the stars,
Stirring embers as the pale moon rises.

Seasons, people, and places fade away.
I miss those talks as the pale moon rises.

There are lessons held in these memories,
If I may ken, when the pale moon rises.

in the chair

hours
in the hundreds
feet up
arm tapped
watching that bag fill with lifeblood
feeling satisfied about helping
others in my own way

all that time donating platelets
did not prepare me for
the three hours I spent with him
during one of his dialysis treatments
my time – a choice
his – a necessity
while I felt helpless
he was

Your Country Roads

After a youth of small towns
and country roads, suburbia
became your home, stayed
your home until you retired,
took yourself back
to country roads that fit you
like a glove worn with pride.
But health has its risks, and pride
has its limits. Blows to your health
meant blows to your pride, took you
back to suburbia, closer to family,
short as that lasted. If your time
had to be up so early, so young,
it should have been on those roads
that fit you so well.

One More Complication

By his side during dialysis,
one more complication,
five months into this hospital stay.
The fear in his voice
unmistakable as he wondered
if this was to be his new norm.
A simple routine before the month
was up. Of no consequence
when the month ended.
When nothing mattered.

One Way or Another

Did you know?
Did you fear?
Did you brush it all aside?

We thought we knew.
But did we understand how short
your time with us would be?

Over the years, they tried to tell you,
but what do doctors know?
Life is for living. For you, to the fullest.

When blood sugar can only be tested
by the doctor, avoid sweets the week before.
You were only fooling yourself.

You knew better in your later years,
but it caught up to you. It was too late.
For all of us, it was too early.

My early years, it turns out,
were your middle years.
Before my middle years, you were gone.

The Last Door

Doctors distant as the city
does not mean illness will not visit
or ignore any door left open
by a lifetime taken for granted.

Medicine is stopgap,
unable to remedy old habits
paused for doctor visits,
resumed until the next appointment.

The future waits,
until it runs its course,
takes its final toll
once the last door is closed.

More Than a Side Trip

A side trip into Buffalo.
Every day.
More than five months.
A twenty-five minute drive
to or from work becomes forty-five.
Inconvenience doesn't fall
to me, but to him.

His hospital stay seems
like forever, at least
to the end of his life.
My visits a mere thirty minutes,
with all the time in the world
ahead of me.

Same parking spot on Oak.
Left side on a one-way street.
Same guy on the same corner.
Every day, holding his cardboard sign
as I approach Buffalo General.
Taking donations, thinks he's got it
bad, but he's not the one inside,
dying, or dying inside with every visit.

That last visit, very early morning
after a middle-of-the-night
phone call that no one wants to get.

Not really a visit, more of a formality.
No one asking for handouts,
just a cold hand that's too hard
to let go and a wish to still have
that daily side trip to or from work.

A Shallow Slope

Mostly level, the yard
that lay before the house,
but sloping past the end of
a ranch nowhere near a ranch,
just a homestead of sorts,
your home in retirement
with a yard that sloped
gently until it reached
the former bank of the creek
that lay another fifty yards
away, the other side of
the valley rising steeply
beyond it, your property line
down the middle of a creek
of few pebbles, mostly
large boulders that impeded
the flow of water but did nothing
to slow time, your time running
short, though you wouldn't
know it until it was too late,
the shallow slope of your lifeline
dropping precipitously
out of sight, out of our lives.

The Second of December

Who calls a wife from the hospital
at 3 am to tell her she's a widow?
My call comes five minutes later
as I prepare for an early shift at work.
My mother tells me she's a widow.
The December morning sky
holds no stars as I drive to her house,
with no stars on any second December
mourning to come. I don't need a phone call
in the middle of the night to tell me that.

Missed in Any Weather

The farthest thing from my mind
when I'm chipping away
at the frozen layer on my driveway
on a typical February morning in Missouri
that has as much rain as snow
is to wish for more of the same.

But here I am on a ninety-six-degree day
in August wading through heat waves
rising from the asphalt outside of Target
that remind me of that hospital parking lot
in Vegas after visiting Dad in June of '93,
his chest reopened, then closed and healing,

and thinking he'd be flying home soon –
we know how that worked out –
wishing I could have one of those
ice-crusted days. Back then it was
crushed ice in his cup, relief
in what was supposed to be his recovery.

When he did come home on Father's Day,
the gurney that rolled out of the air ambulance
held a ninety-year-old man who left
his fifty-nine-year-old-self back in Vegas
and back home meant being back
in a Buffalo hospital with a glass of crushed ice.

I'd give anything to see him once more,
that cup in hand. Better yet, just one minute
working beside him back in the '70s
with the snow blowing between the trailers,
almost drifting across the loading dock,
and his face just as red from the cold

as it would get if he were here with me
on this hot, August Missouri day,
that thought frozen in my mind.

Lost in Time

What is time,
when you are no longer a part of it?

What is time,
when our time with you is in the past?

What is time,
when your years were wiped clean in a moment?

What is time,
when it seems like only yesterday?

What is time,
when it seems so long ago?

What is time,
when missing you seems to fill it?

What is time,
when all we have are memories and dreams?

treasured moments

life well lived
loved by all you touched
memories

final hours
darkness closes in
by your side

bittersweet
treasured last moments
emptiness

moving on
behind, beside you
without you

A Face Well Known

There is no mistaking him,
this image I have
of my father in my youth,
hair thin, thinner even than
mine is sixty years later, but
always in a wave. The same,
thirty years ago, in his last days,
when he had but a few strands
in the front. But the smile
he passed on to me? Every morning,
there is no mistaking him
when I look in the mirror.

This Precipice

Standing on the edge.
Not a transition.
A delineation.
This matter of health
taken for granted,
even with minor setbacks.
Considering how minor
suddenly becomes major
in a body that weathered
past storms, recovery
not the challenge it has become
in an old age that may have come
gradually, but announced itself
with a sudden urgency,
this precipice never once
considered in younger years.

Warped

I walk the walls,
my head around the corner
that lies beyond the door.
Precarious in this chair on the ceiling,
I cling to the fan that should not be
on the floor above me, spinning
me in starts and stops. In a world
of contradictions, I touch nothing
and everything at the same time.

Vertigo, my isolation.

Handicapped Parking

A wheelchair beside the highway,
back wheels on a grassy slope
urging it to roll backwards
a hundred feet to meet
the Ohio River, is no match
for pickups and SUVs with hands
on wheels that steer around
minor hazards, just wants to
rock forward, hands on wheels,
to get back on the shoulder
and get across that highway
without getting hit
or going for a swim.

skin deep

when healing thoughts aren't enough
facing a truth skin deep
means resurfacing old concerns
with another decade of hope
that cancer doesn't return

peel back this layer
find me as I was
as I am
the difference subtle

Pace Yourself

A finger on the pulse of

What?

My own heart?

Those close to me?

The world?

It looks like that ship has sailed.

You could say the world is
wounded, just limping along.

But its heart is also racing,
AFib to the extreme.

I have no idea what will fix it.
It's outpaced me.

My focus…
The pulse of the people
who mean the world to me.

Close to the Heart

Specialists tell me it's not all there, my interatrial sep-
tum. Blood that should be pumped to my lungs to be
filtered may pass through that barrier. Flow in one
direction can cause oxygen-rich blood to join blood
going to the lungs, overtaxing them. Flowing in the
other direction, blood that needs to be filtered by the
lungs will join blood destined for the brain, which can
lead to mayhem.

More than sixty-five years of my life passed before
this was discovered. By a stroke of luck, my one stroke
was minor. When it passed through the hole in my
heart, a tiny clot that could have come from any injury
did reach my brain, but its effect was minor. The hole
can be closed with surgery, but with fewer advantages
due to my age – so I accept this defect as a part of my
whole.

tiny sparrow drinks
from freshly fallen rain
ripples move in rings
leave unknown repercussions
echoes that wait to be heard

A Missed Beat

Transient, as in there.
And not.

Or just a memory   lapse?
Followed by   another.

And another.
How to block that flow?

How to learn what you already know?

What is the name for this?
Or this?

Here.   Gone.

Wake up the next day.   Wonder
what that was all about.

Try to remember why you couldn't.
Hope it wasn't the first of many.

Go with the Flow

Blood flows,
knows
where it should go,
sometimes goes
where it wants.

Take my PFO.
Please.
That hole in my heart
that lets blood flow
where it shouldn't
sent a clot to my brain,
the strain minor.
This time.

Or the bruises
on my arms.
Everywhere.
Spatial orientation
gone to hell
since that TIA.

The blood thinner
to stop those clots?
It whispers to my blood.
There's fresh air
beyond that skin.

Go for it!

And minor cuts, or
just plain scratches?
Let's just say
I've used more band aids
in the last year
than I have
in the previous 69.

Like I said,
blood knows
where it wants to go.

Pissed

at all this medical shit
rolling downhill
as I go downhill
never getting ahead

Privacy

In the public sector
Pharmacy, two open registers
A line stretches down the aisle
Customers step forward
One after another
Stand at the counter
Side by side
Name, date of birth
Questions about a prescription
Loud enough for the world to hear
We value your privacy

synchronicity

unforeseen illness
takes words in new direction
author now subject
newfound consideration
for the gift of each moment

now understanding
all that I experience
both past and present
share same space as the future
all held in the same moment

Feeding an Addiction

A simple shopping errand,
groceries,
but never one
to pass on a chance
to write a poem,
he cooks up a new malady
and takes a side trip
to the ER.
Pancreatitis.
Waiting on a room
for the night,
he searches for words.
There has to be a better way.

dehydration distillation

thought process
distillation
dehydration
expectation contingency
ER-r on the side of caution
symptoms stated
emergency modulated
locked down like
a fortress of discomfort
in the eye of the holder of the keys
RN/ing the show
no admission without
an admission of election
options limited
wait it out
or
wait it out
impatient patients
clock watchers
with no clock to watch

Juggling Act

Up and down.
All around.
Which one is it?
This one? That one?
What about this?
Round and round
and round we go.
Maybe it's the pancreas.
No, that's back to normal.
Gallbladder. That's looking dicey.
Or the liver. That's off the charts,
and not in a good way.
Throw in AFib and a fever,
and sleep on it. Take two aspirin
and call me in the morning.
My bill is in the mail.

The Bruiser

Slight
Skinny, actually
Definitely not a bruiser
Athletics limited to softball
and sandlot football
Until someone sees speed
in that wiry frame
A sprinter, no less,
but still no muscle
to speak of – well, enough
later to get the job done
But time marches on,
and slight becomes not-so-slight
Health issues set in
A TIA and a hole in the heart
that might explain some things
Then anemia, and more layers
added to a frame far from wiry
And blood thinners
Oh, those blood thinners,
and the bruises appear
Stubbed toes turn blue
Bumps into door frames
bring yellow elbows and arms
Hips glow orange, fingers rosy
with the smallest scrape or cut

A week-long hospital stay,
and arms and hands become
pin cushions as the bruiser
shows his true colors

One-Hit Wonder

They may be one hell of a trio,
but they only have one memorable tune,
a one-hit wonder of angst and pain.

Gallbladder, stoned out of its mind,
lets one rip long enough to send
Pancreas into a shrieking fit.

Not to be outdone, Liver responds
with an infectious laugh
that borders on manic.

It's clear that Gallbladder has to go
but can't be cut from the act
until Liver settles down.

So, what's up with Liver, fear of failure?
Never been mistreated, never been
one drink away from destruction.

But if Gallbladder stays stoned,
destruction is inevitable,
and no one wants to hear that tune.

Nothing but Time

Time / Pink Floyd

The clock ticks,
as it always does.
An alarm rings,
or does it?
There hasn't been one
dull day, as alarms
have been going off
for the past week.

Doctors think they know,
but do they?
So they send me on a road trip,
my gurney boosted
into the back of the bus.
It's hard to believe
I now call this my hometown,
but I leave it behind
as we head into the night.

Looking back at headlights,
taillights, I wonder
if I've frittered, wasted
the years that are behind me.
But no one was going to show me,
so I made my own way.

I've lived each moment,
and nothing can take that from me.

I once was young,
and life was always long.
Until it wasn't.
But that doesn't mean
that each day doesn't have
its own starting gun.

Waters and Gilmour may not
expect me to catch up with the sun,
but I know it's waiting,
offering me a new day. I'll always be
older, and I may be short of breath,
but death will have to wait.
I'll take every minute, every
scribbled line that comes my way,
save them, learn from them
until I'm finally home.

It's just past midnight as we pull up
to the hospital in St. Louis.
I know my past is always
a part of me, but this is a new day
and I'm ready to make more memories.

bus ride

mid-Mo
to STL
the quickest, not
necessarily the smoothest,
route for riding
on one's back

where's the suspension,
when a crate of eggs
couldn't survive
126 miles
of what fragile
organs have to rely on?

great attendants on that trip,
but two hours later
has this rider thinking
he'll walk home
if his own wheels
are not available

Pallbearer

Should I damn you,
unnamed cursewielder,
that you have chosen this time
to burden this simple agebearer?
Though the years ahead grow shorter,
my healthburden has not
weighed so heavy as to cast a pall
upon my prospects. Yet, one blow
from you, a healthstrike
from out of the blue, has dimmed
my view of what awaits me.
Perhaps this is just one more
lifechapter, one that, once it passes,
will serve to remind me of
the power of your lifegrasp.

Wayback Machine

Don't ask me how I got here
Eyes open or closed
It was all the same
Lights passing in the night
Headlights, taillights
Every seam in the road
Lifting me
Dropping me
Maybe if I'd tried to
Count them
Listen to them
Let them tell me where I was
I'd know how to get home
Instead of lying in a tunnel
That goes nowhere
As it hums and whirs, thuds
With a bass that holds no beat
Yet knows me better than I do
Sees the real me
Only to return to stare at walls
And out a window that tells me
Nothing about the way back
If there is a way back

Dulcet Tones Do Not Lessen the Impact

Vital signs on display.
BP   Pulse   O2
Soft tone gently
reminds me to take slow,
deep breaths. When did breathing
become such a conscious effort?
COPD is new this year,
but never to this extreme.
Then the doctor says
pneumonia. Already
compromised in the hospital,
should I be surprised,
when it hangs out here,
thinks this is a resort?
The people here may be nice,
but I can think of better places
to listen to soft, gentle tones.

beyond the pane

a bird on the ledge
tapping on the glass
not a glass of iced tea
the glass of a window
looking in on me
nine stories up
as I sip iced tea
and think about a bird
that's not there
but thinks I must have
better things to do
little knowing painkillers
will take the mind places
far beyond the imagination
of a bird that's not there

sweet 16

days
maybe not so
sweet

favorite hospital
is there such a thing?
30 miles away

local ER
compromise
not really capable

complications
always a possibility
require better care

transfer required
favorite now an option
that's not available

off to St. Louis
same system as
compromise

with a reputation
that fits my needs
126 miles from home

hospital beds
and hospital floors
my new norm

a waiting game
fighting infection
home soon, they say

only to return
in another month
for surgery

16 days
and counting
not really so sweet

It Could Be Worse

Helluva way to get to St. Louis,
not that I got to see much more than
headlights and taillights for two hours
as the ambulance drove me into the city.
Two weeks of staring at
the medical school across the street
wasn't much better, the only relief
the morning mist over the Mississippi,
Illinois on the horizon.

The place never did grow on me,
but one thing became clear.
When one doctor said to prepare
for the worst, then sent me here,
those who know better taught me
what that doctor should have known.
Cancer's not on my horizon.
I may have something to worry about,
but it could have been a helluva lot worse.

Road to Recovery

126 miles home and
you feel like you could walk
every one of them, but you know
you won't make it into the first.

Pack your bags. Make that one.
It may be 18 days, but the clothes
you started with will get you home.
Load it into the truck.

You're a passenger today,
first time in a very long time.
Seat back, feet up.
You have a long ride ahead of you.

Freddie Freeloader

Freddie Freeloader / Miles Davis

Slow and lazy, Miles' horn
opens the tune, subtle
bass, piano, and percussion
nudging it along as I climb
into the truck, passenger side,
a rare occasion. Anesthesia
doing its best to hang on, though
wearing off as we drive away
from the surgery center,
wants to hold onto that horn
as long as possible.

Piano takes over, a conversation
about my procedure, details
rattled off as if I remember
any of it, but a percussive beat,
fingers snapping me out of it,
reminds me I'm just waking up.

The horn seems to wake up
as we head for a late lunch.
Twenty hours after my last meal,
I feel the hunger gnawing at me,
Coltrane and Adderly on sax
adding impetus. Piano, bass,
and percussion come out front

to lead into the horn, smooth,
but punctuated by sax
as Freddie Freeloader exits and
I leave the truck for some chow.

Softening the Blow of Galling News

Four incisions,
sewn on the inside,
speak to me through
the glue on the surface,
tell me to taste life
in a new way. Through
my post-surgery meal
I see that taste has not
changed, absent a gallbladder,
but know it now colors
the way I consider my options,
sheds new light on my choices.

Inspiration Where You Can Find It

for Ron.

Clinics and waiting rooms.
He says they offer some of the best
inspiration. Thoughts go
where you least expect,
or maybe where you'd expect,
but in ways least expected.

Mine did, but I'm not sure
if it was because of the way
they snuck up on me
during eighteen days of
oxygen and adjustable beds or
if it was the distance from home.

Nothing seems to have changed,
now that I'm back. Is it because
I know there will be more clinics
and waiting rooms? If I ever see him,
I'll have to ask. I just hope
it's not in a waiting room.

Scarred for Life

Scan after scan.
Procedure after procedure.
But the one that counted?
On hold,
waiting for the chance
to remove the one thing
with the gall to put this
whole thing in motion.
Nine months
to be clear of infection
before that bad boy was
finally sucked out of there,
then two more months
to fully heal. The only evidence
of a yearlong medical marathon
that started with eighteen days
in the hospital? Four tiny scars.

Singin' in the Rain

one umbrella
two umbrellas
wrapped around a hole
that's the way
the doctor says
to fix a PFO

your blood should pass
around your heart
and not have a loophole
that will be fixed
when I am done
I aim to make it whole

so cross your heart
and hope that I
know what I am doing
and if by chance
this doesn't work,
well, there's always gluing

The Whole Story

Holed up in a sterile room,
held up by all that tran-
spired on a mourning
that failed to deliver
desired results, I stare
at the ceiling, the most
that I can get out of
this failed operation
a web of inexplicable
expectations that were
never guaranteed and
leave me scarred
for a life that's no different
than the one I knew
when I entered. No leg
up on the situation,
nothing changed, nothing
gained, I leave behind
any hope for resolution,
wonder why I even bother.

Empty Spaces

I approach nothing as if a threshold,
always just before me. Little separation
but thoughts and memories.
Indistinct, then gone without notice.

Is there meaning in absence,
as my days grow shorter
and my thoughts slip away?
What is a memory that cannot be held?

Leaves will fall from a maple.
See its shape. Imagine the spaces filled,
and you will not be disappointed
when spring returns.

My spring is behind me.
It is my spaces that grow,
with less to fill them
as they approach that threshold.

Don't Lose Heart

To the heart of the matter
Have a heart
Know this by heart
Take heart
Wear your heart on your sleeve
Whole-heartedly
Straight from the heart
Take it to heart
Heart is normal sized
Follow your heart
Know this with all your heart
Find it in your heart
To your heart's content
Your heart is in the right place
Keep it close to your heart
Anxiety gnaws at the heart
You may have a change of heart
The heart size is enlarged
Don't lose heart
You still have a heart

The Same, but Different

Not all that different
Okay, different

Easy childhood for me
For him, not so much

Eighth grade,
the farthest he got

University for me,
two years – almost

Blue-collar, Teamster,
on both counts

Medical issues
always in his face

What medical issues?
Almost nonexistent for me

Act as if that doesn't matter
A way of life for him

Worried that it matters for him
Thankful it doesn't for me

Almost old
when it caught up to him

Older, now, and missing him
My issues start piling up

We couldn't be more different
Why do I feel so much the same?

Timeless Machine

No rewind

To change
a heart with a hole in it
from birth

Or change
one kidney, half-sized
from birth

Too late to rewire

a brain
that changes channels
faster than any remote

Too much time spent
looking for the remote

Too early
to let the clock run down

Nothing to do but let it play
until the clock runs down

Any Day, Every Day

Take me

Shake me

Stand me up

Against any wall

Bedroom

Hotel

Hospital

This IV in my arm

Straight to my heart

You give me life

You give me all the love

I'll ever need

Final Release

When dotage arrives,
in the winter of my years,
surround me not with four walls.

Rather, set me free,
to feel the freshest of air
flow through my very core.

Let my weary bones become one
with the simplest of forces
that beckon us all.

A Simple Gesture

Need I say already
when so much time has passed,
when each passing moment
seems to take moments with it?

Sight and sound blurred
and muffled, impressions
that bring new meaning each time
my mind tries to repeat them.

Amentalio. The word would be
foreign to you, but I can imagine
your reaction to it, that gesture
not lost to me, yet. A shrug,

the slightest tilt of your head,
followed by a question.
How can you forget something
that is such a part of your soul?

Amentalio: the sadness of realizing that you're already forgetting sense memories of the departed- already struggling to hear their voice, picture the exact shade of their eyes, or call to mind the quirky little gestures you once knew by heart.

-*The Dictionary of Obscure Sorrows,* John Koenig

Ken Gierke (on the right) is a transplanted Western New Yorker, moving in retirement to mid-Missouri in 2012. He is a Pushcart Prize nominee, and his poetry has appeared in numerous anthologies. His poetry collections, *Glass Awash* in 2033, *Heron Spirit* in 2024, and *Random Riffs* in 2025, were published by Spartan Press.

This project was made possible, in part, by generous support from the Osage Arts Community.

Osage Arts Community provides temporary time, space and support for the creation of new artistic works in a retreat format, serving creative people of all kinds — visual artists, composers, poets, fiction and nonfiction writers. Located on a 152-acre farm in an isolated rural mountainside setting in Central Missouri and bordered by ¾ of a mile of the Gasconade River, OAC provides residencies to those working alone, as well as welcoming collaborative teams, offering living space and workspace in a country environment to emerging and mid-career artists. For more information, visit us at www.osageac.org

www.ingramcontent.com/pod-product-compliance
Lightning Source LLC
Chambersburg PA
CBHW022229160726
47991CB00016B/2661